DEDICATED TO YOU

May this book bring you love and joy for your entire existence.

SHIVA : He is the Beginning, the Middle and the End

CONTENTS

Foreword

In the vast tapestry of literature, there emerges a work that transcends the ordinary and beckons readers into a realm where the profound meets the extraordinary. It is with great pleasure that I introduce you to **"Shivaksh: Unleash Your Inner Shiva,"** a captivating creation by the Emerging and spiritually aligned author.

Within these pages, a journey unfolds—one that goes beyond the boundaries of conventional storytelling. "Shivaksh" invites you to embark on an odyssey, guiding you through the uncharted territories of self-discovery, resilience, and the untapped reservoirs of inner strength.

The title **"Shivaksh: Unleash Your Inner Shiva,"** encapsulates the essence of this transformative narrative. Much like the deity it draws inspiration from, the book encourages readers to delve deep within themselves, exploring the facets of their
own inner Shiva— a source of power, resilience, and enlightenment.

As you traverse the narrative landscape meticulously crafted by me, you will encounter characters and situations that mirror the complexities of our own lives. Themes of self-discovery, empowerment, spiritual growth resonate throughout, inviting introspection and a profound connection with the story.

"Shivaksh" is not merely a book; it is an invitation to embrace the extraordinary within the ordinary.
May this book serve as a guide, encouraging you to unleash your inner Shiva— to confront challenges with unwavering strength, to navigate the labyrinth of existence with grace, and to ultimately discover the limitless potential that resides within.

ACKNOWLEDGEMENTS

As I pen down the final pages of **"Shivaksh: Unleash the Inner Shiva in Me,"** I am filled with gratitude and humility for the incredible journey that has led to this creation. This endeavour has been a mosaic woven with threads of inspiration, resilience, and the unwavering support of those who have touched my life in meaningful ways.

To the cosmic forces that guided my hand and fueled my imagination, I express my deepest appreciation. The divine energy that flows through the universe has been a wellspring of inspiration, shaping the essence of **"Shivaksh."**

To my family, whose love and encouragement have been the bedrock of my creative pursuits, thank you for standing by me through every chapter of this journey.

A heartfelt appreciation goes to my friends and mentors who have provided valuable insights and encouragement. Your wisdom has been instrumental in shaping the narrative of **"Shivaksh."**

I extend my gratitude to the readers who embark on this adventure with open hearts. It is my sincere hope that the pages of "Shivaksh" resonate with you on a profound level, inspiring you to unleash your inner Shiva and embrace the transformative power within.
Special thanks to my mother
Ms Jyoti Chandnani, whose directions added a unique dimension to this work. My parents' thoughtful guidance has been invaluable. I am blessed to have such incredible support systems in my life.
I am truly fortunate to have such talented and motivated students, and their involvement has been instrumental in shaping the outcome of this work.

To my sister **Ms Sona Chand**, thank you for being my rock and for always believing in my abilities.

To my best friend **Ms Sheena Malhotra**, your willingness to lend an ear and offer feedback have been instrumental in shaping the direction of this book.

In the spirit of self-discovery and shared growth, I dedicate **"Shivaksh: Unleash the Inner Shiva in Me"** to all seekers of inner strength, wisdom, and spiritual awakening. May this book be a beacon of inspiration on your own journey of self-realisation.

Introduction

LEARNING, FEELING & KNOWING

The feeling of knowing or being known is an internally generated feeling of knowing that ensures a phenomenological sign of goal attainment and has as its consequence the termination of thoughts, ideas, or actions motivated by concerns of harm to self or others.

Intuition is that sense of knowing what the right answer or decision is before you make it. It's a deep, internal, visceral feeling. You know your intuition is around when you say things like, "I can't really explain it, but..." or "It just felt right" or, more likely, "It just felt wrong."

SHIVA : He is the Beginning, the Middle and the End; He is the Past, the Present and the Future.

The journey to Shiva helps you to surrender yourself . It ensures to find utmost, pure love, understanding and compassion for oneself.

The world is full of material possessions, lust, success and credit.

Shiva shows us what to do in a world that is obsessed with success, lust, credit, and material possessions. We should own up to our mistakes and move forward.

Third Eye: Shiva has the third eye, through which he sees everything, whether it be in the past, present, or future. However, he is still regarded as **Bholenath.** SHIVA was the one who first put this seed into the human mind. According to the yogic lore, over fifteen thousand years ago, Shiva attained to his full enlightenment and abandoned himself in an intense ecstatic dance upon the Himalayas. When his ecstasy allowed him some movement, he danced wildly. This book depicts my journey of surrendering and having an utmost, pure love, understanding, and compassion for self and for all.

The Path to Enlightenment begins with Self-Discovery

The journey of finding and exploring one's own thought process, ideas, rationality, values, compassion and opinion is SELF DISCOVERY. Knowing your own self: mind and soul. Self-reflection is an elemental prerequisite for self-discovery since it allows an individual to spend a substantial amount of time alone to figure out the main purpose of life. Self reflection works wonders in solitude. With ongoing thoughts and chaos in mind, no one can find the purpose of life. Multiple questions and their answers could only be figured out in solitude. Let those dust particles get settled in your mind to get a better picture and clarity of oneself.

Once upon a time a young brahman approached a pleading for help with his anger problem. "I have a quick temper, and it's damaging my relationships," the young brahman said.

"I'd love to help," said the saint. "Can you demonstrate your quick temper to me?"

"Not right now. It happens suddenly," the young man replied.

"Then what is the problem?" asked the saint. "If it were a part of your true nature, it would be present all the time. Something that comes and goes is not a part of you, and you shouldn't concern yourself with it."

The man nodded in understanding and went on his way. Soon afterwards, he was able to become aware of his temper, thus controlling it and repairing his damaged relationships.

Your emotions are not you but they can gain control over you if you do not reflect on them. The only way to tame a subconscious reaction is to bring the light of consciousness to it. Once you become conscious of a belief, action or emotion, it no longer wields control over you. Self-discovery is the foundation of self-awareness. By exploring one's thoughts, emotions, and motivations, individuals gain a clearer understanding of who they are. Self-Understanding often involves accepting and embracing imperfections. It recognizes that enlightenment is not about achieving perfection but about understanding and integrating the complete self.

In Hindu philosophy, especially within the context of Shaivism, Lord Shiva, often referred to as Mahadeva or the Great God, is considered the embodiment of ultimate reality and supreme consciousness. The teachings and stories associated with Mahadeva in various scriptures, including the Mahashivpurana, provide insights into how individuals can attain enlightenment or spiritual awakening through devotion and understanding of the divine nature.

Destroyer of Ignorance (Avidya)

Mahadeva is often depicted as the destroyer of ignorance and illusion. Through devotion and surrender to Shiva, individuals seek the removal of ignorance that veils the true nature of reality. The destruction of ignorance is seen as a step towards enlightenment. The idea of Lord Shiva as the "Destroyer of Ignorance" is a recurring theme in many Hindu scriptures, including the Mahashivpurana. While the term "destroyer" may sound forceful, in the spiritual context, it refers to the dissolution of ignorance and illusion that veils the true nature of reality.

Destruction of Ego (Ahankara)

The stories of Lord Shiva often involve his disregard for personal ego and material attachments. Devotees learn from Shiva's example to transcend ego and material desires, recognizing that enlightenment comes when one goes beyond the limitations of the self. The concept of overcoming ego is deeply embedded in the broader teachings of Shaivism and Hindu philosophy.

Once, the demon Andhaka, born blind, was granted eyes by Lord Shiva due to the demon's penance. In return for the boon, Andhaka promised not to harm anyone who showed kindness to him.Andhaka grew powerful and began to think of himself as invincible.

Fueled by his ego, he developed an infatuation with Parvati, the consort of Lord Shiva. He sought to possess her by force, ignoring her pleas and the fact that she was already married to Shiva.In the heat of the battle,Lord Shiva, in his form as Virabhadra, severed Andhaka's head with a swift strike. However, to everyone's surprise, each drop of Andhaka's blood that touched the ground transformed into a new Andhaka. The battlefield became crowded with countless Andhakas.To address this situation, Shiva adopted a brilliant strategy. He assumed the form of Ardhanarishvara, a composite androgynous form of Shiva and Parvati. In this form, Shiva absorbed the essence of Parvati into himself, creating a harmonious union of male and female energies.

Shiva, now in the Ardhanarishvara form, revealed the true nature of Andhaka's existence and the futility of his ego-driven pursuits. Andhaka, humbled and enlightened, surrendered to Shiva. Acknowledging his arrogance and realizing the divine truth, Andhaka sought forgiveness. Impressed by Andhaka's transformation and sincerity,Shiva granted him a boon. Instead of being killed repeatedly, Andhaka asked for liberation through divine knowledge (jnana). Pleased with his humility and newfound wisdom, Shiva blessed Andhaka with liberation.

The story of Andhaka emphasizes the destructive nature of unchecked ego and the transformative power of surrender to a higher spiritual truth. Lord Shiva, as the destroyer of ego, not only humbled Andhaka but also granted him liberation through wisdom and self-realization.

This narrative illustrates the profound spiritual teachings embedded in Hindu mythology, emphasizing the importance of humility, self-awareness, and the dissolution of ego on the path to enlightenment.

CHANNELLING YOUR INNER SHIVA VIBES

Channelling your inner Shiva vibes involves connecting with the qualities and symbolism associated with Shiva. Here are some practices and mindset shifts that may help you tap into your inner Shiva.

Lord Shiva manifests as Dakshinamurti, the divine teacher, who imparts profound wisdom to a group of sages in a silent yet powerful manner.

Dakshinamurti sits under a banyan tree in absolute silence. The sages, eager to learn, gather around him. Without uttering a word, Dakshinamurti imparts knowledge through the stillness of his being, transmitting the essence of Atma Jnana through profound silence.

The banyan tree represents the expansive universe, and Dakshinamurti, as the silent teacher, symbolises the supreme knowledge that transcends words. Through his divine presence, the sages attain a direct realisation of the self beyond the limitations of verbal teachings. The story underscores the importance of inner contemplation and the direct experience of the self. Dakshinamurti's teachings emphasise that self-knowledge is not merely intellectual but requires a profound inner realisation.

PRACTISE MEDITATION AND STILLNESS

Shiva is often associated with meditation and stillness. Set aside time for daily meditation to quiet your mind and connect with your inner self. Focus on your breath, and try to achieve a state of inner calmness. The key is to create an intention of stillness — to have some intentionality about how we're carrying ourselves in a given moment — and to focus on what is within our control. Stillness looks different at different moments and in different situations .For example, the ultimate "best" still moments are when I turn off the stimuli around me, such as the television and radio. I might shut my eyes to calm my thoughts and focus my attention on one thing. I try to make the moment "as basic and simple as possible." For instance, you might physically slow down by sitting, slowly walking, or even lying down, she said. You might reduce external stimuli in your environment by lowering the lights and turning down

the music.

DANCE AND MOVEMENT

Shiva's cosmic dance, known as the Tandava, symbolises the rhythm of creation and destruction. Engage in dance or rhythmic movements to connect with the dynamic and ever-changing nature of life. The psychology of dance is the set of mental states associated with dancing and watching others dance.

YOGA PRACTISE

Incorporate yoga into your routine, especially poses that represent Shiva's attributes. The Tadasana (Mountain Pose), for example, can evoke the strength and stability of Shiva.

Before you go ahead with asanas and exercises, try to clearly define why you want to practise yoga. It could be for physical fitness, stress relief, flexibility, spiritual growth, or a combination of these.

SYMBOLIC IMAGERY

Lord Shiva is often associated with various symbolic imagery that carries deep spiritual and cultural meanings. Surround yourself with symbolic imagery associated with Shiva, such as the trident, the crescent moon, and the third eye. These symbols can serve as reminders of the qualities you seek to embody.

1.Third Eye (Trinetra): Lord Shiva is often depicted with a third eye, symbolising higher perception, knowledge, and insight beyond ordinary sight. It represents the ability to see the truth beyond the physical and material world.

2.Crescent Moon (Chandra): Shiva is sometimes shown wearing a crescent moon on his head. The moon represents the passing of time and the cyclic nature of creation, preservation, and destruction.

3.Snake (Naga): A serpent adorns Shiva's neck, symbolising the control over the forces of desire and ego. It also represents the Kundalini energy, a powerful spiritual force believed to reside at the base of the spine.

4.Ganges River (Ganga): The flowing Ganges river is often depicted flowing from the topknot of Shiva's hair. It symbolises purity, life, and the divine flow of cosmic energy.

5.Blue Throat (Neelkanth): The epithet "Neelkanth" (blue-throated) refers to the legend of Shiva consuming the poison during the churning of the ocean (Samudra Manthan) to save the world. His blue throat symbolises the acceptance and transmutation of negative forces.

6.Damru (Drum): Shiva is often portrayed holding a small drum called a damru. The rhythmic sound of the damru represents the heartbeat of the universe, and its two-sided nature symbolises the dual aspects of creation and destruction.

7.Ashes (Bhasma): Shiva is smeared with ashes (bhasma), symbolizing the transient nature of material life and the ultimate reality of death. It also represents the renunciation of worldly attachments.

8.Tiger Skin (Vyaghra Charma): Shiva is sometimes depicted sitting or standing on a tiger skin, symbolising victory over lust and control over the primal instincts.

9.Trishul (Trident): Shiva carries a trident representing the three fundamental aspects of existence: creation, preservation, and destruction. It also symbolises the three gunas (qualities) of nature – sattva, rajas, and tamas.

10.Damaru (Sacred Drum): The damaru is a small drum tied to the trident, representing the rhythmic sound of the cosmic energy. It is associated with the creation of the universe through the sound of the primordial vibration (Om).

These symbolic elements collectively convey profound spiritual teachings and insights associated with Lord Shiva's role in the cosmic cycle of creation, preservation, and dissolution. They also highlight the importance of transcending worldly attachments and realising the impermanence of material existence.

CHANTING AND MANTRAS

Mantras are sacred sounds, syllables, or phrases that are believed to have spiritual and transformative powers. Here are some popular mantras dedicated to Lord Shiva.

Om Namah Shivaya (ॐ नम: शवाय)
Translation: **"I bow to Shiva."**

This is one of the most widely known and powerful mantras dedicated to Lord Shiva. It is a five-syllable mantra that represents the five elements and is considered a potent mantra for meditation and spiritual awakening.

Maha Mrityunjaya Mantra
Om Tryambakam Yajamahe Sugandhim
Pushtivardhanam Urvarukamiva Bandhanan Mrityor
Mukshiya Maamritat

ॐ ह   जं ूस: ॐ भूभुव: व: ॐ   य बकं
यजामहेसुग पु वधन म्ॱ उवा क मव ब ना मृ योमुीय
मामृतात्ॱॐ व: भुव: भू: ॐ स: जं ू ह ॐ

Translation: "We worship the Three-eyed Lord Shiva who is fragrant and who nourishes and nurtures all beings. May He liberate us from death, for the sake of immortality, as the cucumber is severed from its bondage.

Shiva Gayatri Mantra
Om Tatpurushaya Vidmahe Mahadevaya Dhimahi
Tanno Rudrah Prachodayat
ॐ तत्पुरुषाय विद्महे महादेवाय धीमहि तन्नो रुद्रः प्रचोदयात

Translation: "Om, Let me meditate on the great Purusha, Oh, greatest God, give me higher intellect, and let God Rudra illuminate my mind."

Shiva Panchakshara Stotram

Nagendraharaya Trilochanaya Bhasmanga ragaya
Maheshvaraya Nityaya Shuddhaya Digambaraya
Tasmai Nakaraya Namah Shivaya

नागे -हाराय -लोकानाय भ म-अंगगा-रागया महे[ए- तीय]
राय | न याय शु ाय दग-अंबराय त मैन_काराय नमः शवाय

Translation: "Salutations to the one who has a serpent around his neck, three eyes, ashes all over the body, the great lord, eternal, pure, and naked. Salutations to Him, the letter 'Na."

Chanting these mantras with devotion and understanding of their meanings is believed to bring spiritual benefits, inner peace, and blessings from Lord Shiva. It's important to practice mantra chanting with sincerity and focus, and you can choose the mantra that resonates most with you.

EMBRACE CHANGE

Shiva is the lord of transformation and change.
Embrace the impermanence of life and be open to
change. Recognize that endings are often the
precursor to new beginnings.

DESTROY LIMITING BELIEFS

Shiva is the destroyer of illusions and limitations.
Identify and let go of limiting beliefs that hold you
back. Challenge yourself to break free from mental
barriers and embrace your full potential. The
symbolism associated with Shiva can be a source of
inspiration and guidance in overcoming limiting
beliefs.
The image with ash smeared on his body and living
in the cremation ground signifies detachment from
material possessions and ego. By adopting a more
detached perspective, individuals can distance
themselves from the emotional attachments that
often reinforce limiting beliefs.
Shiva is also known as the lord of transformation.
The destructive aspect of Shiva is not about causing
harm but about breaking down the old to make way
for the new. Similarly, by acknowledging and
dismantling limiting beliefs, individuals can undergo
a transformative process, paving the way for
personal growth and positive change.

In the Presence of the Cosmic Dancer, Lord Shiva

Unfolding oneself in the presence of the cosmic dancer, Lord Shiva, involves a journey of self-discovery, transformation, and alignment with the cosmic forces. The process of finding oneself is a time taking process. Approach it with patience, sincerity, and an open heart. By aligning yourself with the cosmic dancer, Lord Shiva, you may discover new dimensions of your own being and experience a profound connection to the universe.

In the presence of the cosmic dancer, Lord Shiva, one is invited to a sacred and transformative space. Picture yourself within the cosmic dance, surrounded by the rhythmic movements that echo the eternal pulse of creation and dissolution.

As you stand in the presence of Lord Shiva, feel the vibration of the cosmic dance reverberating through your being. The dance is not merely a physical expression but a manifestation of the cosmic energy that flows through the universe. It is the dance of life, the dance of creation and destruction, the dance of the eternal cycle.

Close your eyes and allow the dance to draw you in. Sense the ebb and flow, the rise and fall of energies within and around you. The third eye of Lord Shiva, representing wisdom, opens within you, bringing clarity and insight. In this dance, the boundaries of the self begin to dissolve, and you become attuned to the universal rhythm.

As the cosmic dancer, Lord Shiva, moves gracefully, envisioning the serpentine energy, Kundalini, awakening within you. Feel it rising along your spine, unlocking dormant potentials and connecting you to the higher realms of consciousness. The dance becomes a journey of self-discovery, a movement toward inner illumination. In the presence of the cosmic dancer, Lord Shiva, you are invited to surrender to the divine flow. Let go of resistance, embrace the dance of life, and allow the cosmic energies to guide you on your spiritual journey. As you dance with Lord Shiva, you become a reflection of the divine dance, a unique expression of the cosmic rhythm. Once, there was a celestial gathering of deities and sages in the heavenly realms. As they marveled at the grandeur of the cosmos, a divine presence emerged. Lord Shiva, in his form as Nataraja, the Lord of the Dance, appeared. As the cosmic drums resounded, Lord Shiva began his celestial dance, the Ananda Tandava, the Dance of Bliss. With every movement, the universe came into existence, sustained by the rhythm of his dance. The cosmic dance symbolized the eternal cycle of creation, preservation, and destruction.

Symbolism of the Dance:

Creation (Srishti): Shiva's dance creates the universe, with each movement giving rise to galaxies, stars, and all forms of life.

Preservation (Sthiti): The balanced postures of the dance represent the preservation and sustenance of the cosmic order.

Destruction (Samhara): The fierce aspects of the dance signify the inevitable destruction and dissolution of all things.

In the sacred town of Chidambaram, there stood a grand temple dedicated to Lord Shiva as Nataraja. The town was immersed in divine vibrations, and pilgrims from far and wide gathered to witness the cosmic dance.

Devotees believed that witnessing Nataraja's dance at the Chidambaram temple bestowed divine blessings and liberation. It was said that in the presence of the Cosmic Dancer, the illusions of the material world faded away, and the devotees were drawn into the rhythm of the divine dance.

Pilgrims would often enter a trance-like state, experiencing a profound spiritual awakening in the presence of Nataraja. The dance became a metaphor for the journey of the soul, transcending the limitations of the physical body and connecting with the infinite.

Seeking Solace in Shiva's Divine Embrace

In the quiet sanctuary of my heart, one will always find refuge, seeking solace in Shiva's divine embrace. Like a weary traveller returning home, one will turn inward, drawn to the tranquil depths where the cosmic energy of Lord Shiva resides.

With eyes closed, one breathes in the essence of the sacred, allowing the soothing vibrations of "Om Namah Shivaya" to permeate my being. In this meditative space, the tumult of the external world fades away, and honestly I am enveloped by the stillness that Shiva's presence brings.
As one will navigate the dance of his own existence, he will find reassurance in knowing that, like Shiva, one always holds the power to transform challenges into stepping stones and to embrace the ever-changing rhythm of life.

The warmth of Shiva's divine embrace wraps around us, a gentle reminder that we are not alone on this spiritual journey. The trident held by Shiva symbolises the power to overcome, to pierce through illusions, and to navigate the complexities of existence. As we surrender to Shiva's embrace, we will definitely feel a release—an unburdening of worries and a deepening sense of inner peace.

The crescent moon adorning Shiva's locks illuminates our path, removing the shadows of doubt and uncertainty. In Shiva's embrace, we find clarity—a guiding light that leads us towards self-discovery and spiritual awakening.

As we seek solace in Shiva's cradle, we will be reminded of the sacredness of letting go. Like the flowing waters of the Ganges, the divine river that finds its source in Shiva's locks, we will release attachments and cleanse our spirit. In this surrender, we shall become receptive to the divine grace that flows unconditionally.

In the presence of Shiva, time loses its grip, and I am anchored in the eternal now. The past fades, the future becomes a distant horizon, and all that remains is the divine moment. Here, I find solace—not in the absence of challenges, but in the unwavering strength and serenity that Shiva imparts.

In seeking solace in Shiva's embrace, I discover an existing sanctuary within, where the eternal dance of the cosmos continues, and I am an integral part of the divine choreography.

25

Awakening the third eye through devotion to Mahadeva

Awakening the third eye through devotion to Mahadeva is a deeply personal and spiritual journey. It involves a combination of inner exploration, dedication to spiritual practices, and a sincere connection with the divine.

Authentic and sincere devotion is at the core of awakening the third eye. It involves a deep love, reverence, and surrender to Mahadeva. A genuine desire to connect with the divine and seek spiritual growth is the foundation of this journey. Consistent and regular spiritual practices create a conducive environment for the awakening of the third eye. Daily rituals, meditation, mantra chanting, and other devotional practices build a routine that nurtures spiritual growth.

Creative visualisations involving Mahadeva, the third eye, and divine light can stimulate the awakening process. Imagining the third eye opening like a blossoming flower or envisioning Mahadev's presence can enhance the connection with the spiritual realm.Regular introspection and contemplation on one's spiritual experiences contribute to self-awareness.

Reflecting on the inner journey and the insights gained helps individuals understand their progress and align with the divine purpose.The journey of awakening the third eye through devotion to Mahadev is a transformative process which also requires patience that unfolds at its own pace. It requires patience, dedication, and a deep inner commitment to the spiritual path.

Markandeya, a devoted young sage, undertook severe penance to seek the grace of Lord Shiva. His intense devotion attracted the attention of Mahadeva.

To test Markandeya's devotion, Shiva appeared in the form of a fiery Linga (an abstract representation of the divine) surrounded by flames. The Linga's heat became unbearable, but Markandeya remained steadfast in his worship.

Unable to bear the intensity of the Linga's heat, Markandeya dived into it with unwavering faith. To everyone's astonishment, including the deities witnessing the scene, Markandeya emerged unscathed from the Linga.

As a reward for Markandeya's exceptional devotion, Lord Shiva blessed him by opening his third eye. With this awakened eye, Markandeya gained the ability to perceive the subtle dimensions of reality and divine truths.The opening of the third eye granted Markandeya profound insights and intuitive knowledge. He became a revered sage, sharing his wisdom with others and guiding them on the path of devotion and self-realization.

Devotion Transcending Obstacles: Markandeya's unwavering devotion to Mahadeva symbolizes the idea that genuine and steadfast devotion can transcend even the most challenging circumstances. **Opening of the Third Eye:** The story highlights the awakening of the third eye as a divine blessing, symbolizing heightened perception, spiritual insight, and a deeper connection with the divine.

Intuitive Wisdom: The third eye is associated with intuitive wisdom and the ability to perceive truths beyond ordinary perception. Markandeya's newfound abilities exemplify the transformative power of divine grace.

Lesson in Devotional Persistence: The narrative encourages devotees to persist in their devotional practices, even when faced with difficulties. The opening of the third eye becomes a metaphor for the spiritual rewards of steadfast devotion.

Bhrigu, a revered sage, was deeply devoted to Lord Shiva. His intense yearning for a direct vision of Mahadeva led him to undertake rigorous penance and austerities.

Bhrigu chose the sacred Mount Kailash, the abode of Shiva, as the site for his penance. For years, he engaged in severe meditation, focusing his mind and heart on the worship of Lord Shiva.

To test Bhrigu's devotion, Lord Shiva, in the form of a simple ascetic, appeared before him. Ignoring the sage, Bhrigu continued his meditation, immersed in the image of Shiva he held in his heart. Undeterred by Shiva's apparent indifference, Bhrigu intensified his penance. He remained steadfast, offering his devotion to the unseen, formless Shiva, represented only by the image in his mind.

Impressed by Bhrigu's unwavering dedication, Shiva revealed his true form and blessed the sage. As a result of his devotion, Bhrigu's third eye, the eye of wisdom, opened, granting him profound insight and spiritual vision.The opening of the third eye signifies the awakening of inner vision, enabling Bhrigu to perceive the divine reality beyond the limitations of the physical senses.

People, inspired by these teachings, strive for an inner awakening that transcends the ordinary and leads to a heightened state of consciousness symbolized by the awakened third eye. In essence, the concept of awakening the third eye through devotion to Mahadeva is more of a symbolic and spiritual journey rather than a literal narrative found in the scriptures.

It involves a deep connection with the divine through sincere and unwavering devotion, leading to inner transformation and spiritual illumination.

Drenched in the Serenity of Shiva's Meditation.

Engaging in meditation inspired by Shiva's serenity can be done at any time that suits your schedule and preferences. However, some individuals find specific times of the day or occasions more conducive to spiritual practices.

Early Morning (Brahma Muhurta)

Traditionally, early morning, during the Brahma Muhurta (around 4:00 AM to 6:00 AM), is considered auspicious for spiritual practices. The mind is generally calmer, and the environment is quiet, providing an ideal setting for meditation.Meditating during Brahma Muhurta, which is the early morning period approximately one and a half hours before sunrise, is considered auspicious in many spiritual traditions, including those rooted in Hinduism and yoga. Here are some potential benefits and beliefs associated with meditating during this sacred time.

1.Increased Sattva Guna: According to Ayurveda and Hindu philosophy, there are three gunas or qualities that influence human nature: Sattva (purity), Rajas (activity), and Tamas (inertia). Brahma Muhurta is believed to be dominated by Sattva Guna, making it an optimal time for spiritual practices, including meditation. It is thought that the mind is naturally calm and receptive during this period.

2.Enhanced Focus and Concentration: The early morning hours are often quieter, with less external noise and distractions. Meditating during Brahma Muhurta may provide an environment conducive to deep concentration and heightened awareness.

3.Alignment with Circadian Rhythms: The body's circadian rhythms are naturally attuned to the rising sun. Meditating during Brahma Muhurta aligns with these rhythms, and it is believed to harmonise the body and mind with the natural cycles of the day.

4.Increased Prana (Life Force Energy): It is said that during Brahma Muhurta, the cosmic energy is at its peak. Meditating during this time is believed to enhance the flow of prana in the body, promoting overall well-being and vitality.

5.Spiritual Progress: Many spiritual practitioners believe that engaging in meditation or other spiritual practices during Brahma Muhurta accelerates spiritual progress. The mind is considered more receptive to higher states of consciousness during this sacred time.

6.Calming Influence: The stillness of the early morning hours is thought to have a calming influence on the mind. Meditating during Brahma Muhurta may help reduce stress and promote mental clarity.

During Sunset

Evening, particularly during sunset, can be another tranquil time for meditation. As the day winds down, the atmosphere tends to be more serene, allowing you to immerse yourself in a peaceful state of mind.

Before Bedtime

Engaging in Shiva's meditation before bedtime can help you relax and clear your mind. It can be a way to end the day with a sense of tranquillity and connection to the divine.

Special Occasions

You may choose to perform this meditation during special occasions related to Lord Shiva, such as Maha Shivaratri or during the month of Shravan. These times are considered spiritually significant, and your practice may feel more aligned with the energy of these occasion.

When Stressed or Anxious

Whenever you feel stressed, anxious, or in need of inner peace, taking a few moments to meditate on Shiva's serenity can be beneficial. It can help you center yourself and find calmness amid life's challenges.

It's important to note that the benefits of meditation can be experienced at any time of the day, and the efficacy of your practice is influenced by your dedication, sincerity, and consistency. While Brahma Muhurta is considered a spiritually potent time, the essence of meditation lies in the regularity and depth of your practice, irrespective of the specific time chosen.

Walking the path guided by Shiva's Cosmic Wisdom

Walking in the path guided by Shiva's celestial wisdom involves integrating the principles and teachings associated with Lord Shiva into your daily life. Here are some suggestions to help you align with Shiva's cosmic wisdom.

Study Shiva's Teachings

Read and study scriptures and texts associated with Lord Shiva, such as the Shiva Purana and other philosophical texts. Understand the deeper meanings and teachings embedded in these scriptures. Studying Shiva scriptures can be a rewarding and enriching spiritual journey. Identify the key scriptures associated with Lord Shiva. Some important texts include the Shiva Purana, Linga Purana, Rudra Samhita of the Shiva Purana, and the Mahabharata (which contains the Shiva Sahasranama) Gain insight into the historical and cultural context of the scriptures. Understanding the background helps in grasping the deeper meanings and symbolism embedded in the texts.

Break down your study into manageable sections.Many scriptures are extensive, so it's helpful to study them systematically, chapter by chapter or section by section. Utilise online resources such as websites, forums, and digital libraries that provide access to translations, commentaries, and discussions related to Shiva scriptures.

Cultivate Inner Stillness

Embrace moments of silence and stillness in your daily routine. Practice meditation to quiet the mind and connect with the cosmic wisdom within.

Once, in a quiet village nestled in the mountains, there lived a wise sage renowned for his deep spiritual insight and inner stillness. People from far and wide sought his guidance on the path to inner peace.

One day, a young and restless disciple approached the sage, eager to learn the secret of state of mind. The sage invited the disciple to join him in a journey to a nearby waterfall.

As they reached the roaring waterfall, the sage asked the disciple to observe the turbulent water. "What do you see?" he inquired.

The disciple replied, "I see chaos, disorder, and relentless movement."

The sage nodded and handed the disciple a small boat. "Now, go into the heart of the waterfall and row."

The disciple hesitated, fearing the strong currents. However, with the sage's encouragement, he rowed into the midst of the turbulent waters.

Despite the chaos around him, the sage remained on the shore, watching intently. After some time, the disciple returned, dripping wet but with a calm expression on his face.

The sage asked, "What did you learn?"

The disciple, catching his breath, responded, "In the midst of the turbulence, I found a point of stillness within myself. The chaos of the waterfall did not disturb my inner peace."

The sage smiled knowingly and said, "Just as the water finds stillness beneath the surface turmoil, so too can your mind find tranquillity amidst the chaos of life. Cultivate the inner stillness that resides within you, and you will navigate life's challenges with grace."

The disciple, now understanding the profound
lesson, continued to study under the sage, learning
to access the reservoir of inner stillness within him.
As he embraced this wisdom, he discovered that
external circumstances need not disturb the serenity
that lies at the core of one's being.
Just like the calm depths beneath a turbulent
waterfall, inner stillness can be discovered within,
even in the midst of life's challenges. Through
spiritual practice and self- discovery, one can
cultivate a reservoir of peace that remains
untouched by external disturbances.

Regular self-reflection, spiritual practices, and a commitment to embodying these principles will help you align with the profound wisdom associated with Lord Shiva.

41

A Glimpse of Eternity in the Eyes of Mahadev

Experiencing a glimpse of eternity in the eyes of Mahadev (Lord Shiva) involves cultivating a deep spiritual connection and engaging in practices that align with the essence of Shiva's transcendental nature.

In a quaint village, there lived a skilled weaver named Govind. Despite his mastery in crafting intricate fabrics, Govind felt a longing within, a yearning for something beyond the tangible threads of existence. Drawn to the nearby temple of Lord Shiva, he sought solace in prayer.

One day, as Govind sat weaving at his loom, a celestial light enveloped him. The loom seemed to transform into an ethereal dance, echoing the cosmic rhythms. To his astonishment, Lord Shiva manifested before him, his eyes reflecting the universe's infinite expanse.

"Govind, you have woven the threads of your life with skill and devotion. What do you desire?" Shiva's voice resonated.

Overwhelmed by the divine presence, Govind bowed and expressed his deepest yearning — to glimpse the eternity within Shiva's eyes. In response, Mahadev touched Govind's forehead, opening his inner eye to the cosmic truth.

As Govind closed his eyes, he saw the universe unfolding — galaxies colliding, stars being born and extinguished, and the dance of creation and destruction. He felt the pulse of existence, transcending the limitations of time and space.

When he opened his eyes, Govind found himself back at his loom, yet forever changed. The patterns he wove now echoed the cosmic dance he witnessed in Shiva's eyes. Villagers marvelled at the graceful beauty of his creations, sensing a divine presence in every thread. Govind, the weaver who glimpsed eternity in the eyes of Mahadev, became a source of inspiration. People from far and wide sought his guidance, not just for the craftsmanship he offered but for the profound stillness that radiated from him — a stillness born from the eternal vision he received. And so, Govind continued to weave not only fabrics but also the threads of divine wisdom into the tapestry of existence, leaving an everlasting mark on the hearts of those who encountered his creations. It emphasises the transformative power of divine experiences and how they can infuse the ordinary aspects of life with profound meaning and purpose. Practice self-inquiry and introspection and surrender your ego and individual identity in the vastness of the divine. Allow yourself to dissolve into eternal consciousness.

Glimpsing eternity is a profound and personal experience, and it may come as a result of dedicated spiritual practice, devotion, and a sincere longing for a deeper connection with the divine. Approach these practices with humility, reverence, and an open heart.

Finding Strength in Shiva's Resolute Calmness

In a picturesque village nestled at the foothills of the Himalayas, there lived a humble priest named Dev. Dev's devotion to Lord Shiva was untiring, and the villagers often sought solace in his wise counsel during times of trouble.

One monsoon, a fierce storm descended upon the village. Torrential rains flooded the fields, and the villagers feared for their crops and homes. Seeking guidance, they turned to Dev.

As the storm raged on, Dev retreated to the small Shiva temple at the village's edge. With an oil lamp flickering in the corner, he began chanting the sacred mantras dedicated to Lord Shiva.

The villagers, huddled together in fear, observed Dev's calm demeanour. His eyes reflected a resolute tranquillity, akin to the calmness found in the depth of a serene lake.

Curious, a young boy approached Dev and asked, "How can you be so calm when the storm is so fierce?"

Dev smiled and beckoned the boy to join him. In the centre of the temple, there was a lotus flower floating in a small bowl of water. Dev pointed to the lotus, "Observe, my child. The lotus thrives in muddy waters, yet its petals remain untouched and unstained."

He continued, "Just like the lotus, we can find strength in the resolute calmness within, even amidst life's storms.

Lord Shiva teaches us to navigate challenges with grace, like the lotus untouched by the chaos around it."

As Dev chanted, the villagers, inspired by his serene presence, began to see the storm in a new light. Instead of fearing the turbulence, they embraced the strength that emerged from their own resolute calmness.And so, in the heart of the storm, Dev and the villagers found solace not in the absence of challenges but in the unwavering strength that emanated from within. The resolute calmness, inspired by their devotion to Lord Shiva, became a guiding light through the tempest of life.

In the aftermath of the storm, as the sun emerged from behind the clouds, the lotus in the temple bloomed with newfound radiance, symbolising the enduring strength found in the resolute calmness inspired by Shiva's timeless teachings.

Shiva's role as the Lord of Destruction signifies the transformative power of challenges. Just as Shiva gracefully navigates the cycles of creation and destruction, individuals can find strength by facing life's challenges with resilience, adaptability, and grace.

Bowing to the Destroyer of Negativity, Lord Shiva.

Bowing to Lord Shiva helps one to discover the transformative power of letting go, finding strength in surrender, and allowing the destroyer of negativity to pave the way for a brighter, more colourful existence.

Once there lived a skilled weaver named Kavi. Despite his talents, Kavi harboured resentment and negativity in his heart. His envy of others' success overshadowed his craft, leaving his once-vibrant creations dull and lifeless.

One day, Kavi learned about a renowned sage visiting the village who was said to possess the power to dispel negativity. Seeking redemption, he approached the sage with a heavy heart.

The sage, perceiving Kavi's inner turmoil, suggested a pilgrimage to a sacred Shiva temple a top a distant mountain. "Bowing to the destroyer of negativity, Lord Shiva, will cleanse your heart," the sage advised.

Eager for transformation, Kavi embarked on the journey. The ascent was arduous, reflecting the challenges within. Upon reaching the temple, he was struck by its simplicity and the divine aura surrounding the Shiva Lingam.

With a heavy heart, Kavi bowed before the sanctum, praying for release from the negativity that consumed him. As he surrendered his burdens, a profound stillness enveloped him. In that sacred moment, he felt a weight lifted from his soul.

On his descent, Kavi noticed a change within himself. His once-muted creations now bore the vibrancy of newfound positivity. Villagers marvelled at the transformation, and Kavi's art became a source of inspiration for all.

Bowing to the destroyer of negativity, Lord Shiva, had not only cleansed Kavi's heart but had revitalised his craft, turning his work into a beacon of beauty and resilience.Overcoming negativity with an inclination towards Mahadev (Lord Shiva) involves combining spiritual practices, mindset shifts, and practical strategies. Some suggestions to help you navigate through negativity with the guidance of Mahadev.

Develop mindfulness to recognize when negativity arises. Acknowledge your thoughts and emotions without judgement. Awareness is the first step towards transformation. Cultivating awareness in the aegis of Mahadev is not limited to specific moments but can be integrated into various aspects of your daily life. It is a continuous practice that can lead to a heightened sense of spiritual connection, self-awareness, and inner peace.

In moments of negativity, consciously invoke the presence of Mahadev. You can do this through prayer, chanting mantras, or visualising the image of Lord Shiva. Feel the divine energy helping you overcome challenges.If you have a Rudraksha mala, you can use it to count repetitions of Mahadev's mantra, such as "Om Namah Shivaya." The tactile experience can deepen your connection and concentration.

Surrender your worries and negative emotions to Mahadeva. Offer them with humility and trust that divine energy can transform your challenges. Surrendering doesn't mean giving up but allowing a higher power to guide you. Surrender, in a spiritual context, involves letting go of control, trusting a higher power, and accepting divine guidance.

When negativity or feelings of despair persist, and you've tried various approaches without relief, surrendering to Mahadeva can be a way to release burdens and trust in the transformative power of divine intervention. Acknowledging your own limitations and understanding that there are aspects of life beyond your control can be a signal to surrender. Surrendering doesn't imply weakness but rather a recognition of the need for divine assistance. Surrendering to Mahadeva involves a continuous letting go and trusting in the divine unfolding of your journey.

Exploring the Infinite Facets of Mahadev's Grace

Exploring the infinite facets of Mahadev's grace is often motivated by a deep spiritual yearning and various personal factors.A genuine desire for spiritual growth and a quest for deeper meaning in life can lead individuals to explore the infinite facets of Mahadev's grace. The search for a higher purpose and connection with the divine is a powerful motivator.

In a bustling city, there lived a compassionate soul named Meera. Moved by the suffering around her, Meera dedicated her life to serving the less fortunate. One day, exhausted and disheartened by the enormity of the task, she sat by the river, seeking solace.

As she gazed at the flowing waters, an elderly sage approached. He spoke of Mahadev's infinite grace and how it flowed like a river, touching every corner of existence. Inspired, Meera decided to explore this divine river of compassion.

She began her journey by helping the homeless, feeding the hungry, and comforting the grieving. Each act of kindness was a step closer to the source of Mahadev's grace. One day, as she sat in meditation, she felt a profound connection with the divine river within.

In moments of stillness, Meera experienced the infinite facets of Mahadev's grace—a gentle current of love, a powerful stream of strength, and the soothing waters of solace. The more she explored, the more she realised that Mahadev's grace was not distant but an ever-present flow within her own heart. Meera's journey became a testament to the boundless compassion that Mahadev bestowed upon the world. The river of grace, she discovered, was not just an external force but an internal awakening—a recognition of the divine within and the infinite facets of Mahadev's grace that flowed through every act of love and kindness.

Putting it all together, the expression "Exploring the infinite facets of Mahadev's grace" implies a profound spiritual journey. It suggests a quest to understand and experience the various dimensions of the divine grace bestowed by Lord Shiva.

This exploration may involve seeking insights, wisdom, and transformative experiences that arise from a deep connection with the spiritual essence represented by Mahadeva.

Devotees and seekers on a spiritual path often engage in practices such as meditation, prayer, and contemplation to connect with the divine and explore the boundless aspects of grace. The journey is seen as a continual process of discovery and spiritual growth.

Understanding the interconnectedness of learning, feeling, and knowing is crucial for holistic human development. Learning can lead to knowing, and both can influence our emotional experiences and responses. For example, learning about a subject may contribute to a deeper understanding, and the emotional response to that knowledge can influence subsequent learning and understanding.

In summary, these three elements are intricately woven into the fabric of human experience, influencing how we perceive and interact with the world around us. They represent key dimensions of cognition, emotion, and awareness that contribute to our overall sense of self and our engagement with the complexities of life.

Feeling is associated with the emotional aspect of human experience. Emotions can be influenced by external stimuli, thoughts, or physiological responses. Understanding and managing emotions is an essential aspect of emotional intelligence. Knowing combines cognitive understanding with a sense of certainty or awareness. It can involve intuitive knowledge, intellectual comprehension, or experiential insights. Knowing goes beyond mere information; it often includes a deeper understanding or a sense of conviction.

Karma as the Rhythm, Dharma as the Melody – Harmonising Existence with Divine Purpose.

Karma is a concept that originated in Hinduism and Buddhism. It refers to the law of cause and effect, stating that every action has consequences. Positive actions lead to positive consequences, and negative actions lead to negative consequences. In the context of your analogy, karma as the rhythm implies the regular and repetitive nature of actions in life. Like the steady beat of a rhythm, karma suggests a continuous cycle of actions and their corresponding outcomes.

Dharma is a complex and multifaceted term. In Hinduism, it generally refers to one's duty, righteousness, or moral and social obligations. In Buddhism, it is often associated with the teachings of Buddha.If karma is the rhythm, dharma as the melody suggests a harmonious and purposeful expression of life. Dharma guides individuals in leading a righteous and fulfilling life, much like a melody adds depth and meaning to a musical composition.

In music, harmony is the combination of simultaneously sounded musical notes to produce a pleasing effect. In the context of your analogy, harmonising existence implies finding a balance and alignment between one's actions (karma) and the moral and social principles (dharma).This suggests a connection with a higher, transcendent purpose or cosmic order. The idea is to align one's actions and duties with a larger, meaningful purpose, creating a harmonious existence.

In the context of life, the melody represents a consistent and harmonious guiding force. It embodies the ethical and moral principles that individuals choose to follow. This refers to the quality of being morally right or just. The melody of righteousness suggests a guiding tune formed by adhering to principles that promote goodness, justice, and virtue.

The inclusion of moral and ethical principles adds significance and depth to the actions and choices made in life. Instead of mere routine, there is purpose and intention behind each action, contributing to a more profound and meaningful existence.

Once upon a time, in the sacred land of Varanasi, there lived a humble musician named Raj. He was known for his extraordinary talent in playing the sitar, and his melodies had the power to touch the souls of those who listened. Despite his musical prowess, Raj was a man of simplicity and integrity. One day, as Raj strolled along the Ganges River, he encountered an old sadhu who seemed to radiate wisdom. The sadhu, with a long white beard and a trident in hand, was none other than Lord Shiva, the divine deity who embodied both destruction and creation.

Once upon a time, in the sacred land of Varanasi, there lived a humble musician named Raj.

As the years passed, Raj's fame spread far and wide, and people from distant lands travelled to Varanasi to experience the transformative power of his music. Yet, despite his success, Raj remained grounded, always remembering the guidance of Lord Shiva.
In the twilight of his life, as Raj played his final notes, Lord Shiva appeared before him once again.
"Raj, your life has been a harmonious blend of karma and dharma. Your music has become a timeless symphony, echoing the divine purpose of existence. Now, join the cosmic dance and let your soul merge with the eternal rhythm."
And so, Raj transcended into the cosmic dance, leaving behind a legacy of music that continued to inspire generations, a testament to the profound wisdom of karma and dharma, guided by the divine presence of Lord Shiva.

The harmonious dimension arises when there is a consistent alignment between one's actions and the ethical principles guiding those actions. Like the harmonies in music, where different elements come together seamlessly, the integration of righteousness creates a harmonious flow in life. This concept acknowledges the cyclic nature of actions and consequences. Each action sets off a series of events, and the interplay of these actions and their outcomes forms a rhythmic pattern. The inclusion of the melody of righteousness ensures that this rhythmic interplay is guided by ethical considerations.

Conscious and Intentional Living

Awareness: Being conscious involves staying present and aware in the moment.

It means understanding the impact of your actions and choices on yourself and others.

Intentionality: Living with intention means making choices that align with your values and goals. It involves thoughtful decision-making rather than merely reacting to circumstances.

Ethical Considerations

Values and Principles: Ethical considerations are rooted in personal and societal values. This involves reflecting on principles such as honesty, integrity, compassion, and justice, and incorporating them into decision-making.

Ethical living involves considering the potential consequences of actions on oneself and others. It takes into account the broader impact of choices on the well-being of individuals and the community.

Contributing to Beauty and Depth

Beauty in Actions: Ethical actions, driven by values and mindfulness, contribute to the beauty of human interactions. Acts of kindness, empathy, and compassion create a positive and uplifting environment.

Depth in Relationships: Ethical living fosters deeper connections with others. Trust and mutual respect are built on a foundation of ethical behaviour, enhancing the quality of relationships.

Transformative Rhythm that Alleviates our Earthly Burdens

The transformative rhythm that alleviates our earthly burdens, as symbolised by Lord Shiva, lies in the understanding and acceptance of the cyclical nature of life. Lord Shiva, in his celestial dance, represents both the destructive and creative forces of the universe. His dance signifies the perpetual cycle of creation, preservation, and dissolution.

This transformative rhythm teaches us that suffering and challenges are inherent aspects of life. By acknowledging and embracing these challenges, we align ourselves with the natural flow of existence. The dance of Shiva invites us to release attachments, transcend limitations, and find resilience in the face of adversity.

Furthermore, Shiva's third eye, the eye of wisdom, sees beyond the surface of transient difficulties. It perceives the eternal truth that suffering is temporary and, in its transformative dance, provides an opportunity for growth and evolution.

In essence, rhythm is about recognizing the impermanence of suffering and understanding that, just as Lord Shiva's dance transforms the universe, our trials can lead to inner strength and spiritual growth. By attuning ourselves to this celestial rhythm, we gain the power to navigate through life's challenges with grace, finding peace amid the storms and alleviating the burdens that weigh on our earthly existence.

In the sacred town of Ujjain, there lived a weary farmer named Keshav. His fields, once lush and abundant, now struggled under the weight of drought and unpredictable weather. Every day seemed like a relentless battle against the forces of nature, leaving Keshav burdened with worries that etched lines on his face.One night, as Keshav lay beneath the starlit sky, unable to find solace in sleep, he heard a distant drumbeat. It was rhythmic and hypnotic, as if the universe itself had composed a melody to ease the burdens of the earth. Intrigued, Keshav followed the enchanting sound, and it led him to the outskirts of the town. There, beneath an ancient banyan tree, sat a venerable sage. His eyes sparkled with wisdom, and in his hands, he held a damaru - the sacred drum of Lord Shiva. The sage greeted Keshav warmly and spoke, "Dear farmer, the rhythm of this drum holds the key to alleviating earthly burdens. Come, sit beside me, and let the beats guide you to liberation."With a heart heavy with concerns, Keshav hesitated but eventually joined the sage beneath the banyan tree. As the sage started playing the damaru, a rhythmic pulse enveloped the surroundings. Keshav closed his eyes, allowing the beats to permeate his being.

In the rhythmic trance, Keshav experienced a profound connection with the earth and the celestial realms. He saw the cycles of life and death, the dance of creation and destruction, all synchronised with the beats of the sacred drum. His burdens seemed to dissolve, replaced by a sense of harmony that resonated deep within.

As the drumbeat gradually faded, Keshav opened his eyes to find the sage smiling. "You have glimpsed the life changing rhythm of Lord Shiva," said the sage. "Take this understanding back to your fields, and you shall witness the earth responding to the cosmic dance. Play the rhythm in your heart, and watch as it transforms your struggles into a harmonious flow." Empowered by the sage's teachings, Keshav returned to his farm. Inspired by the cosmic rhythm he had experienced, he began to cultivate his fields with a newfound awareness. He played a simple drum to the beat of his heart, infusing the soil with the energy of Lord Shiva's moves.

Miraculously, the weather patterns shifted, and rains blessed Keshav's land. The once barren fields now yielded a rich harvest, and the townspeople marvelled at the transformation. Keshav's rhythmic connection with the universe had brought prosperity not only to his farm but to the entire town of Ujjain.

Word of Keshav's story reached the far corners of the land, and people from all walks of life sought the wisdom of the rhythmic farmer. Under the ancient banyan tree in Ujjain, the beats of Lord Shiva's transformative rhythm continued to echo, offering solace and liberation to those burdened by the challenges of earthly existence. And thus, the drumbeat of liberation resounded through the ages, a timeless melody that carried the promise of transformation to all who listened with open hearts.

The concept of a rhythm that curtails earthly burdens is often metaphorical and symbolic, drawing inspiration from spiritual and philosophical perspectives. It involves finding practices and rituals that resonate with your own experiences and contribute to a sense of balance and well- being.

A life-transforming song that alleviates earthly burdens can have profound effects on our well-being and mental state. Here are several reasons why music, particularly a transformative song, holds the power to make a significant positive impact on our lives.

In essence, the association between Lord Shiva and the transformative rhythm that reduces earthly burdens lies in the profound symbolism of his celestial dance, the rhythmic beats of the damru, and the spiritual practices that align individuals with the dynamic flow of the universe. Devotees turn to these aspects of Shiva's symbolism and teachings seeking inner transformation and relief from the challenges of earthly existence.

The Serenity of a Heart Aligned with Truth

The calmness of a heart aligned with truth is like a tranquil river, unwavering in its course. In the stillness of honesty, ripples of peace gently embrace the shores of the soul. Let truth be the current that guides your journey, and you shall navigate life's waters with the calm assurance that the riverbed of your heart remains unshaken by the storms of deception. In the serenity of truth, find solace, find strength, and let the authenticity of your being flow, a source of endless, undisturbed tranquillity. The poise of a heart aligned with truth is a state of inner peace and calmness that arises when one lives in accordance with their authentic values and principles. Achieving this serenity involves cultivating a mindset and lifestyle rooted in honesty, integrity, and authenticity.

In a world often characterised by excess and constant stimulation, choosing a life of simplicity and minimalism becomes a deliberate and transformative choice. The journey begins by decluttering the physical space around you. Assess your belongings and let go of items that no longer serve a purpose or bring genuine joy. This act of simplifying your surroundings creates an environment of calm and order, promoting a sense of clarity in the midst of the chaos.

Beyond the tangible, simplicity is also a state of mind. Streamlining daily routines, commitments, and relationships becomes paramount. Identify the essential aspects that contribute positively to your life and well- being, and gracefully let go of the rest. This mental decluttering allows for greater focus on what truly matters, fostering a deeper appreciation for the present moment.

Minimalism extends to mindful consumption. Instead of pursuing an abundance of possessions, shift the focus to quality over quantity. Be intentional in your choices, seeking items and experiences that align with your values and bring lasting satisfaction. As you adopt a minimalist mindset, you'll likely find that the pursuit of material possessions is replaced by a quest for meaningful experiences and connections. Reflect on your values and aspirations, allowing them to guide your decisions. Embrace the philosophy that less can indeed be more, finding contentment in the simplicity of a purpose-driven life. By simplifying, you create space not only in your physical environment but also in your schedule and mindset. This newfound space provides room for personal growth, creativity, and the pursuit of activities that bring true fulfilment.

In the pursuit of simplicity and minimalism, consider each aspect of your life as an opportunity for intentional living. Strive for balance, recognizing that the journey is unique to each individual.

Through the deliberate choices of decluttering, prioritising, and embracing a mindful lifestyle, you pave the way for a life that is full, not of excess, but of depth, purpose, and the profound beauty found in simplicity.

In the sacred town of Varanasi, nestled by the Ganges River, there lived a sage named Parvataraj. Parvataraj was known for his deep wisdom and profound connection with Lord Shiva. His abode was a humble ashram surrounded by a lush grove of ancient trees, where he lived a life steeped in simplicity and minimalism.

One day, a curious disciple approached Parvataraj, seeking the secret to his contentment and serene way of life. In response, the sage began to weave a tale that intertwined the essence of simplicity with the divine presence of Lord Shiva. In his youth, Parvataraj had been a wealthy merchant, surrounded by opulence and excess. Despite his material abundance, he felt a growing emptiness within. One night, Lord Shiva appeared to him in a dream, urging him to seek fulfilment not in wealth, but in the simplicity of a purpose- driven life.

Inspired by the divine message, Parvataraj renounced his material possessions and embarked on a journey to the sacred city of Kashi. There, he found solace beneath the banyan trees, where he decided to establish his ashram.The grove became his sanctuary, a living testament to the beauty of simplicity.

In the sacred town of Varanasi, nestled by the Ganges River, there lived a sage named Parvataraj. Parvataraj was known for his deep wisdom and profound connection with Lord Shiva. His abode was a humble ashram surrounded by a lush grove of ancient trees, where he lived a life steeped in simplicity and minimalism.

One day, a curious disciple approached Parvataraj, seeking the secret to his contentment and serene way of life. In response, the sage began to weave a tale that intertwined the essence of simplicity with the divine presence of Lord Shiva.

In his youth, Parvataraj had been a wealthy merchant, surrounded by opulence and excess. Despite his material abundance, he felt a growing emptiness within. One night, Lord Shiva appeared to him in a dream, urging him to seek fulfilment not in wealth, but in the simplicity of a purpose-driven life. Inspired by the divine message, Parvataraj renounced his material possessions and embarked on a journey to the sacred city of Kashi. There, he found solace beneath the banyan trees, where he decided to establish his ashram. The grove became his sanctuary, a living testament to the beauty of simplicity.

In the ashram, Parvataraj's daily life revolved around simple rituals and meditations. He owned only the essentials—a saffron robe, a wooden staff, and a small brass bowl for alms. His meagre belongings symbolized a detachment from the material world, allowing him to focus on the spiritual realm and commune with Lord Shiva in the serenity of his sacred grove. Word of Parvataraj's contentment spread far and wide. People from distant lands sought his guidance, drawn to the tranquility that surrounded him. The sage, with his eyes reflecting the wisdom of the cosmos, shared the teachings of Lord Shiva on simplicity and minimalism. He encouraged his disciples to embrace a life of purpose, letting go of the unnecessary burdens that weighed down their souls.

As the sage's disciples followed his teachings, they discovered that true fulfillment lay not in the accumulation of possessions but in the richness of thesoul. The sacred grove echoed with the rhythmic chants of simplicity, becoming a haven for those seeking a path to inner peace and enlightenment. Parvataraj's life became a living hymn to Lord Shiva, embodying the divine principles of simplicity and minimalism. His disciples, inspired by his example, spread the teachings far and wide, creating a ripple effect that touched the lives of countless seekers.

And so, the sacred grove in Varanasi stood as a testament to the transformative power of simplicity —a place where the essence of Lord Shiva's teachings merged with the beauty of a purposeful and fulfilling life. The sage, in his simplicity, became a beacon of light, guiding others on the path to a serene and content existence.

Living a life full of simplicity and minimalism in a world often driven by materialistic pursuits is a conscious and transformative choice that requires a shift in mindset and lifestyle. In the midst of a culture that often equates success with possessions, embracing simplicity means redefining the values that guide one's life. It involves consciously decluttering both physical spaces and mental landscapes, focusing on the essentials that truly bring joy and purpose.

Practising minimalism in a materialistic world doesn't necessarily mean complete deprivation; rather, it encourages thoughtful consumption and intentionalliving. It involves being mindful of the impact of each possession and seeking quality over quantity. Choosing possessions that align with personal values and contribute positively to life's experiences becomes the cornerstone of this lifestyle.

Navigating the materialistic currents of society, individuals on the path of simplicity often find fulfilment in experiences, relationships, and personal growth rather than the accumulation of material wealth. It's about fostering a mindset where possessions serve a purpose and hold genuine value, rather than serving as symbols of status or success.

Living a minimalist life involves letting go of the societal pressure to constantly acquire more and embracing the freedom found in having less. It requires resisting the impulse to accumulate possessions for the sake of appearances and recognizing that true abundance lies in the quality of one's experiences and connections rather than the quantity of belongings. In essence, simplicity and minimalism in a materialistic world become a deliberate act of rebellion against the notion that happiness is derived from the abundance of possessions.

It is an invitation to savour the beauty of a life unburdened by excess, where the focus shifts from what is owned to what is experienced, and where the pursuit of meaning takes precedence over the pursuit of material wealth. It's an intentional choice to create a life that is not defined by possessions but enriched by purpose, mindfulness, and a deep appreciation for the simple joys that exist beyond the realm of materialism.

Convergence of the Relative and Absolute- Essence of Profound Consciousness

The essence of profound consciousness—lies in understanding the dual aspects that shape our perception of reality. Relative consciousness encompasses the intricate interplay of our individual experiences, perceptions, and worldly interactions. It is the lens through which we interpret the tangible aspects of our lives, weaving a complex tapestry of subjective understanding.

On the other hand, absolute consciousness transcends the boundaries of the individual self, representing a timeless and universal canvas that underlies the entirety of existence. It is the profound awareness that connects us all, acknowledging the oneness of the cosmic fabric beyond the distinctions of individual perspectives. Absolute consciousness is the unchanging essence that remains constant amidst the ever-shifting landscape of our relative experiences.

The convergence of these two dimensions occurs when we recognize the inherent interconnectedness between the relative and absolute aspects of consciousness. It is in this recognition that we find the essence of profound consciousness—a harmonious integration of our personal narratives with the universal, eternal truth. By navigating the delicate dance between the relative and absolute, we attain a deeper understanding of our existence, acknowledging the unique colours of our individual threads while appreciating the universal canvas that unites us all in the mosaic of consciousness.

Understanding the convergence of the relative and absolute, the essence of profound consciousness, involves employing various strategies that bridge the gap between individual experiences and universal truths. One key strategy is cultivating mindfulness. By being present in the current moment, we develop an awareness of our subjective experiences, allowing us to acknowledge the relative nature of our consciousness. Mindfulness also opens a gateway to the absolute as it enables us to perceive the underlying unity that transcends individual perspectives.

Another effective strategy is contemplation and reflection. Taking time to ponder the interconnectedness of all things, we can explore the universal truths that anchor our existence. Through introspection, we delve into the absolute aspects of consciousness, recognizing the timeless and unchanging essence that permeates every individual experience.

Engaging in practices that foster empathy and compassion is a third strategy. By understanding and sharing in the perspectives of others, we bridge the gap between the relative and absolute. Compassion becomes the thread that weaves our personal narratives into the larger assortment of collective consciousness, revealing the shared essence that unites us all.

Additionally, the exploration of philosophical and spiritual teachings can deepen our understanding. Wisdom traditions and philosophical insights often provide frameworks for contemplating the convergence of the relative and absolute. These teachings offer guidance on navigating the dual nature of consciousness, unveiling the profound truths that connect the individual with the universal.

Lastly, embracing a holistic approach to knowledge and learning is crucial. By integrating diverse sources of wisdom—scientific, artistic, spiritual—we gain a multidimensional understanding of the convergence of relative and absolute consciousness. This synthesis allows us to appreciate the beauty of diversity while recognizing the common threads that tie us to the universal essence.

Shivaksh Summaries

1.**Self-Discovery:** The book likely emphasizes the importance of self-discovery, encouraging readers to explore their inner selves and understand their true nature.

2.**Spiritual Awakening:** Expect teachings on spiritual awakening, drawing inspiration from the archetype of Shiva, a deity associated with transformation and enlightenment in Hinduism.

3.**Mindfulness Practices:** The book may introduce mindfulness practices and techniques to help readers stay present, reduce stress, and enhance overall well-being.

4.**Inner Strength:** Look for guidance on tapping into inner strength and resilience, fostering a sense of empowerment in facing life's challenges.

5.**Wisdom from Ancient Philosophies:** The author may incorporate wisdom from ancient philosophies, offering a timeless perspective on personal growth and spirituality.

6.**Practical Tools:** Anticipate practical tools and exercises that readers can apply in their daily lives to cultivate a deeper connection with their inner selves.

7.**Symbolism of Shiva:** Learn about the symbolism associated with Shiva and how it can be applied metaphorically to guide personal transformation.

8.**Embracing Challenges:** The book might encourage a mindset shift towards viewing challenges as opportunities for growth and self-improvement.

9.**Connection with the Divine:** Explore teachings on nurturing a deeper connection with the divine, whether it's defined in a religious or more universal sense.

10.**Transformation:** Expect insights on personal transformation, emphasizing the potential for positive change when one embraces their true self and purpose.

May the exploration of your inner Shiva
through this book lead you to the radiant
source of latent happiness that has always
been a part of your authentic self.

Mona Chandnani